The Five-Module Call Center Training System
By Robert Villegas

The Five-Module Call Center Training System

By Robert Villegas

Copyright ©2017 by Robert Villegas. All Rights reserved. No part of this book can be reproduced in any manner without written consent of the copyright holder or his representative/s.

Published in the United States of America

ISBN-13: 978-1979537575

ISBN-10: 1979537577

www.robertvillegas.com

Contact: **robertv1989@outlook.com**

Published by Document Services International

USA

www.documentservicesinternational.com

Table of Contents

THE FIVE-MODULE CALL CENTER TRAINING SYSTEM 4
HOW TO USE THE FIVE MODULE SYSTEM: 6
MODULE 1. – BASIC PROCEDURE AND PLANNED CUE RESPONSES 9
MODULE 2 – REBUTTALS AND COMMON QUESTIONS .. 16
MODULE 3 – VOICE QUALITY 25
MODULE 4. – CUSTOMER PERSONALITY TYPES............. 28
MODULE 5. EARNING CUSTOMER TRUST...................... 32
FINAL NOTE.. 38

The Five-Module Call Center Training System

The Five-Module Call Center Training System is designed to assist the Call Center Team Leader in helping his employees quickly upgrade their skills to an acceptable level. Call Center Representatives are important for the company because, for many callers, they are the only point of contact they will have with the company. Representatives must know the company's quality assurance standards and be able to represent the company well. They often make the difference between a customer with a problem and a customer who will not do business again. Giving proper answers, having the proper attitude and tone of voice are, therefore, of utmost importance for the company.

This booklet will take the Team Leader and employee through a systematic training regimen that will communicate the basic methods for doing the job and ensuring that the representative understands and uses the rebuttals and skills necessary. The Team Leader documents thoroughly all activities and results in order to ensure that the employee is thoroughly trained and understands the job.

This booklet is designed to be focused on the individual and the company should maintain a copy which will be put in the employee's personnel file to document his fulfillment of his job duties.

The system is divided into five modules:

Module 1 Review Basic Procedures

Module 2 Rebuttals and Common Questions

Module 3 Voice

Module 4 Dealing with Customer Personality Types

Module 5 Earning Customer Trust

How to Use the Five Module System:

1. **You can use it as a complete system**
   When used as a complete training system, the Team Leader brings the employee through each Module, not completing a Module until all tools are being used and CPH (Calls Per Hour) results are recorded. This approach can be useful for new people who are struggling and need to improve skills quickly.
2. **You can use the individual modules**
   If a Team Leader has identified a particular area within the five-Module system that needs attention, he/she need only use the Module applicable to the employee's training needs. In this case, it is still important that the Module be fully documented and the CPH results monitored and recorded.
3. **You can use it as a refresher for an experienced person who may have lapsed into bad habits.**
   This approach is similar to #2 above but with a focus on relearning and retraining. Again, it is important that the activities be verified and recorded.

The grading scale is as follows:

1- Not Doing
2- Much Improvement Needed
3- Some Improvement Needed
4- Meeting Expectations

Each module is not complete until the employee has mastered all the skills of the module. The Team Leader should first monitor the call center representative using company-provided monitoring reports and listening equipment before and after each lesson and should perform each step again if not all skills have been put to use. The full process includes:

Step 1. Listen to the representative via monitoring equipment and list the areas in which he or she is not performing their job.

Step 2. Sit with the representative and listen while making note of whether the representative makes the same mistakes with the supervisor sitting with him.

Step 3. Review the results of the calls and inform the representative about those areas where he is performing correctly while the supervisor sits with him compared to when he was being listened to.

Step 4. Discuss with the representative those areas where he was deficient during both sessions and inform him of the correct approach or response and ask that he try those approaches and give the reason why it is important that he respond in the correct way.

Step 5. Sit with the representative again to see if he is using the correct responses and make note of it.

Step 6. Listen with monitoring equipment to see if the representative is using the correct responses and make note of it.

Once all skills have been verified the Team Leader records the latest CPH to determine if the employee has truly made progress. See the form on the next page.

Step 7. Move to the next module and start the process again.

Employee Name	Team Leader and Date

Module 1. – Basic Procedure and Planned Cue Responses

Beginning CPH[1]	Before	During	After

Review the basic procedure when taking an application.

Define the script that the individual uses when making outbound calls. This is the script you are looking for from the representative. Record the script here:

---

[1] Calls per Hour

Full script

Include additional sub-scripts and other responses to look for:

_____
_____
_____
_____
_____
_____
_____
_____
_____
_____

Typical Responses by customer

1. _____
   _____

2. _____
   _____

3. _____
   _____

Typical CSR responses

1. _____
   _____

2. _____
   _____
   _____
3. _____
   _____
   _____

During this module, the Team Leader
  a. Monitors and makes notes on which of the main three areas of the basic procedure they are lacking in.
  b. Thoroughly discusses areas of improvement with the CSR[2] in each of the necessary procedural topics.
  c. Monitor to confirm that the individual is executing the proper procedure when talking with the customer.
  d. Repeat the module nightly until the individual is fully executing each element of the procedure properly.

Parts of the Typical Call
  A. Introduction
     a. Script: Hi, this is _____ with _____. I am calling to _____.
        Qualifying question

---
[2] Customer Service Representative

_____
_____
_____
              ?

Day Used	Grading Scale	Comments
	1 2 3 4	

b. Response to customer statement. Write response/s here

_____
_____
_____
_____
_____
_____
_____
_____
_____

Day Used	Grading Scale	Comments
	1 2 3 4	

B. Application
   a. Records information accurately

Day Used	Grading Scale	Comments
	1 2 3 4	

C. Closure
   a. Identifies self and company.

Day Used	Grading Scale	Comments
	1 2 3 4	

   b. Offers telephone number and address of the company.

Day Used	Grading Scale	Comments
	1 2 3 4	

Ending CPH				

Module 2 – Rebuttals and Common Questions

_____
_____
_____
_____
_____
_____
_____
_____
_____

Beginning CPH				
Beginning CPH				
Beginning CPH				

During this module, the Team Leader
    a. Monitors and makes notes on which rebuttals are not being thoroughly used by the employee while listening in using

monitoring equipment. He also listens in with the employee at his desk to determine if the employee uses the correct script when he is being monitored at his desk.
b. The supervisor discusses with the employee, the rebuttals that need to be used and obtains an understanding and commitment from the employee to use these rebuttals. The key with this sub-module is to ensure that the employee understands why this rebuttal is necessary and how to correctly use it.
c. The supervisor monitors the CSR to confirm that the individual is using the rebuttals required for the job.
d. The supervisor repeats the module daily until the employee is using all the rebuttals.
e. The supervisor monitors and determines if common questions are handled correctly. He asks the CSR to make corrections and re-monitors until all necessary common questions are answered properly.

A. Sample Rebuttals
        a. Not Interested
           - There is no obligation if you don't like our offer.

- _____

- _____

- _____

Day Used	Grading Scale	Comments
	1 2 3 4	

b. I am already satisfied with what I have.
- Do you have any concerns?
- _____
- _____
- _____

Day Used	Grading Scale	Comments
	1 2 3 4	

    c. What rate/price can you give me?
      - I can take down some basic information to see what you qualify for.

Day Used	Grading Scale	Comments
	1 2 3 4	

B. Common Questions
  a. Question:

  _____
  _____?
  - Answer: _____
      _____
  -   _____
      _____
  -   _____
      _____

Day Used	Grading Scale	Comments
	1 2 3 4	

  b. Question

  _____
  _____?
  - Answer: _____
      _____
      _____

- _____
  _____
- _____

Day Used	Grading Scale	Comments
	1 2 3 4	

c. How did you get my phone number?

- _____
  _____
  _____
  _____
  _____
  _____
  _____
  _____

Day Used	Grading Scale	Comments
	1 2 3 4	

d. Where are you calling from?

_____
_____
_____
_____

Day Used	Grading Scale	Comments
	1 2 3 4	

e. Are you going to do a credit check?
   - It shouldn't hurt your credit profile because it is just a soft check and not a hard credit check.
   - _____
     _____
     _____

Day Used	Grading Scale	Comments
	1 2 3 4	

f. I am on the do not call list, why are you calling me?
   - I will put you on our do not call list right now!
   - _____
     _____

_____
_____
_____

Day Used	Grading Scale	Comments
	1 2 3 4	

Ending CPH				

Module 3 – Voice Quality

Beginning CPH				

Voice – Analyze accent, tone of voice, voice quality and professional sound. Monitor, train and re-monitor until all qualities are present in the voice.

Voice Quality	Grading Scale	Comments
Accent	1 2 3 4 5	
Tone of Voice	1 2 3 4 5	
Voice Quality	1 2 3 4 5	
Professionalism	1 2 3 4 5	

If	Then	Comment
Monotonous / Expressionless	Vary pitch and routine. Emphasize key words and phrases. Talk to the person. Listen to someone with a model speaking voice.	
Mumbled words / Voice trails off	Enunciate. Speak directly into the phone. Adjust your level and stay there.	

Speaking too slowly / quickly / Words run together	Match pace. Stress points. Separate beginnings and endings.	
Timid / Unsure	Be the expert. Lower tone. Modify delivery	

Ending CPH				

Module 4. – Customer Personality Types

Beginning CPH				
Beginning CPH				
Beginning CPH				

Listen to how effective the agent is in dealing with different types of customers. Monitor and train until all types are dealt with effectively. Make comments below:

Work Well With All Customer Personalities

Customer Personality	Our Most Persuasive Response
Questioning/untrusting	Confidant professional response. Use facts, figures and examples. Invite questions.
Indecisive/puzzled	Calmly explain and clarify. Voice understanding and concern.
Upset/urgent	Project "in control" authority. Express desire for appropriate solution. Show genuine concern and understanding.

Friendly, helpful	Respond in the same manner. Engage in small talk.
Unsure/uptight	Reassure calmly. Concentrate on benefits. Calmly, slowly lead to conclusion.
Hostile/stubborn	Listen attentively. Calm and confident response.

Ratings

Customer Personality	Grading Scale	Comments
Questioning/untrusting	1 2 3 4 5	
Indecisive/puzzled	1 2 3 4 5	
Upset/urgent	1 2 3 4 5	
Friendly/helpful	1 2 3 4 5	
Unsure/uptight	1 2 3 4 5	
Hostile/stubborn	1 2 3 4 5	

Ending CPH				

Module 5. Earning Customer Trust

Beginning CPH				
Beginning CPH				
Beginning CPH				

Earning Customer Trust. Monitor the employee and evaluate on the following areas:

Building Rapport

	Comments
Listen Actively	
Avoid "Phoniness"	

Relate to the customer as an individual	
Seek the customer's involvement	

Additional Tips and Techniques

	Grading Scale	Comments
Good posture	1 2 3 4 5	
Smile	1 2 3 4 5	
Keep a Rhythm	1 2 3 4 5	
Set a Goal	1 2 3 4 5	

Reward yourself	1 2 3 4 5	

Training Aids

Listen Actively

Be engaging in active listening, you give yourself the best opportunity for success. You also speak with more energy and relevancy. Make your voice clear and respond to the customer's questions right away. Indicate that you are interested.

Avoid "Phoniness"

If it sounds like you are reading a script, the customer will not want to listen. They are too busy to talk to someone who cannot help them and is not interested. Engage them with relevant speech and natural language.

Relate to the Customer as an Individual

If you sound disinterested, the customer will not want to talk to you If you sound like you are "just doing my job," they will know you are "just doing your job." Engage in small talk with the customer. Relate your own experiences where applicable and empathize with their situation Give them hope of giving them something better with your product.

Seek the Customer's Involvement

By getting the customer to relate information, you gain valuable tools for helping them. Ask open questions that start with "Tell me about" or "Explain." Open questions invite answers that give details rather than just a simple "Yes" or "No".

Good Posture

Good posture makes you feel better. It energizes you and prepares you for success. Sit properly and you will succeed.

Smile

When you smile, you have more energy and focus – and you feel better. You should smile before each call and often during the call. Smile after the call and especially reward yourself with a smile if you have a successful call. Some Customer Service Representatives keep a mirror at their desk so they can see themselves smiling to remind themselves of the healing power of a smile. Smile, the customer can hear it.

Keep a Rhythm

Don't languish on a call. If you disqualify the party, get right into the next all before you have time to think about something negative. You keep your workday positive by moving forward and keeping a good rhythm. Keep your fingers poised to disqualify if they are not interested so you can move quickly onto the next all. Remember, you are not going to be successful if you don't move quickly away from those that are not interested. You give yourself a better chance by establishing a good rhythm.

Set a goal.

Every day, you should set a goal for yourself to work toward. This is an important tip for developing focus. Write that goal down and keep it in front of you at all times to help you focus.

Reward yourself

A smile is the quickest reward you an give yourself. After all, you came to work today and that means you will earn money. When you are successful, reward yourself with another smile, or a can of soda, or a gum drop, anything that is pleasurable. If you do extremely well, you may want to reward yourself with a soft drink or even dinner out.

Ending CPH				

Final Note

Every company is different and every project has its unique characteristics. Every script has its specific answers. This book is intended as a general guide that the supervisor must fit into its individual needs. If you would like to develop a work book that deals specifically with your specific client and issues, we would be glad to visit your site and create a training system that deals specifically with your needs. Please contact us by email at **robertv1989@outlook.com** and we will call you back to set up a meeting and develop a quote for you.

- Robert Villegas Document Services International
  www.documentservicesinternational.com

To order additional copies of this book, go to:

http://amzn.to/2hNgeMK

Books on Sport and Entertainment Sponsorship

Finding Sponsors
This book is written for anyone seeking sponsorship relationships in the sport and entertainment fields. The ideas and principles presented here are applicable to any company, sport team, entertainment company, marketing agency and charitable organization that uses corporate sponsorships to support its activities. http://amzn.to/2mflrja $3.49 Kindle $12.95 softcover

Finding Sponsors Forms Book
This "Forms Book is intended to provide samples of the forms mentioned in the book "Finding Sponsors for Sport and Entertainment".
http://amzn.to/2lxnTCF $2.99 Kindle $5.50 softcover

How to Write A Sponsorship Proposal
The goal of this booklet is to provide you with some basic guidelines on what to communicate in order to produce a winning sponsorship proposal.
http://amzn.to/2mPFnKS $2.99 Kindle $7.95 softcover

The Sport Sponsor Handbook
This book is written for companies that would like to explore the benefits of sport and entertainment sponsorship. It is the culmination of years of study, experience and success. http://amzn.to/2mB4K2x $4.49 Kindle $12.95 softcover

Hospitality Event Planning Handbook
How do you pull off a Hospitality Event for your biggest customers? You may not know how to start, what to do and how to ensure the event is a success. This book can help. http://amzn.to/2mxzpgy $7.95 softcover.

www.robertvillegas.com

www.ingramcontent.com/pod-product-compliance
Lightning Source LLC
Chambersburg PA
CBHW071202240526
45470CB00017B/1232